The Most Dangerous Woman in America

by Becky Cheston

Scott Foresman
is an imprint of

Glenview, Illinois • Boston, Massachusetts • Chandler, Arizona •
Upper Saddle River, New Jersey

Photographs
Every effort has been made to secure permission and provide appropriate credit for photographic material. The publisher deeply regrets any omission and pledges to correct errors called to its attention in subsequent editions.

Unless otherwise acknowledged, all photographs are the property of Pearson Education, Inc.

Photo locators denoted as follows: Top (T), Center (C), Bottom (B), Left (L), Right (R), Background (Bkgd)

Opener Bettman/Corbis; **1** Underwood & Underwood/Corbis; **3** (B) Bettman/Corbis; **4** The Granger Collection, NY; **5** Lewis Wickes Hine/Corbis; **6** Library of Congress; **8** Sean Sexton/Corbis; **10** Walter P. Reuther Library; **11** (TL) MPI/Getty Images; **12** ©The Granger Collection, NY; **13** Lewis Wickes Hine/Corbis; **14** Brown Brothers; **16** Lewis Wickes Hine/Corbis; **17** Bettman/Corbis; **19** ©The Granger Collection, NY; **20** Bettman/Corbis; **22** Underwood & Underwood/Corbis.

ISBN 13: 978-0-328-52143-2
ISBN 10:   0-328-52143-4

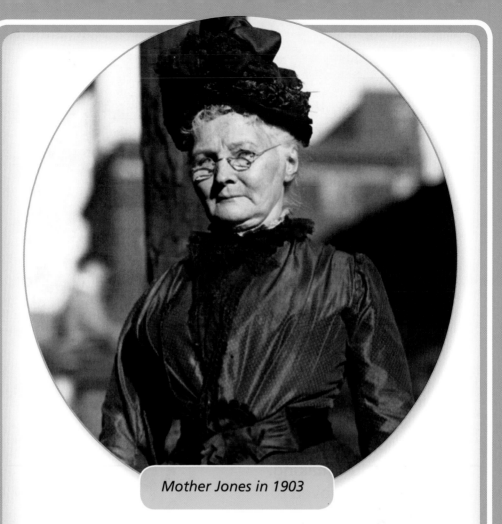

Mother Jones in 1903

Barely five feet tall, she reached down her bony, wrinkled hands to smooth her black dress. Her hat was black, too, with a touch of purple ribbon. Underneath this cap, her thin, white hair, swept into a knot, rested on the back of her neck. This was the so-called "most dangerous woman in America." This was Mother Jones. It was 1903, and she was 66 years old. Her body may have been weak, but the fire in her burned strong. She looked up, her blue eyes scanning the crowd of textile workers. Many of them were children, and all were eager to hear what she had to say. "We march!" she boomed.

A Fighter's Origins

The same Mother Jones who led the march of the textile workers was born Mary Harris in Cork City, Ireland, in 1837. Perhaps she grew up to fight injustice because she witnessed it as a young girl. Britain, which occupied Ireland, kept its soldiers in the streets bullying citizens.

Or perhaps Mary inherited her generous spirit and fiery spunk from her grandfather, an Irish freedom fighter. In any case, Mary's gift for political organizing would not emerge in Ireland, but in the United States. A deadly potato **famine** forced her family to flee to the United States soon after 1840.

Mary spent much of her childhood in Toronto, Canada, and then taught school in Michigan. In her early twenties, she moved to Chicago where she took up dressmaking. In 1861 she moved to Tennessee. It was here that she met and married George Jones, a member of the Iron Workers' Union.

Ireland's Great Famine affected the many impoverished people who depended on the potato for survival.

A Product of Her Times

Mary already possessed the personal qualities that would make her a great leader. The time in which she lived, however, cried out for a "people's fighter." During this era, unions were becoming as vital to a working person as a job itself.

The Industrial Revolution (1820–1870) had transformed how goods were produced. The steam engine was powering a new wave of inventions, such as spinning and weaving machines that allowed goods to be made faster without the need to rest. As these machines sped up the production of goods, workers were brought into the large factories to match this new demanding pace. There were no limits on how many days companies could require people to work, or for how long. The use of child labor was a fact of life.

These **oppressive** conditions led to the birth of the union movement. Mary's husband George Jones was one of many ironworkers who had banded together to fight for higher wages, shorter hours, and more **humane** working conditions. By sticking together for a common cause, union men like George finally had the power to negotiate with management.

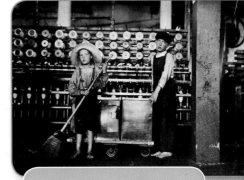

During the Industrial Revolution, children often toiled long days under harsh conditions in factories, mills, and mines.

HARPER'S WEEKLY.

A JOURNAL OF CIVILIZATION.

Vol. XX.—No. 998.]   NEW YORK, SATURDAY, FEBRUARY 12, 1876.   [WITH A SUPPLEMENT. PRICE TEN CENTS.

Entered according to Act of Congress, in the Year 1876, by Harper & Brothers, in the Office of the Librarian of Congress, at Washington.

People warming up over steam outside of a Steam Printing building.

Transformed by Tragedy

Mary and George lived happily together, learning from one another and building a family. However, in 1867, the first of two terrible tragedies struck. An epidemic of yellow fever took hold of Mary's husband and their four children. The disease was so quick and lethal that all five of them were dead within a week. After losing her loved ones, Mary could no longer bear to stay in Tennessee, so she packed up and moved back to Chicago.

Here, Mary once again took up dressmaking. She even opened her own shop. She enjoyed working with her hands, sewing all types of dresses and gowns. Many of the city's wealthiest women took note of her skill. After gaining a reputation for quality work, Mary began to sew for rich Chicago families. She sat in their living rooms stitching custom-made gowns, staring through plate-glass windows to the street outside. Day after day, she saw the jobless and homeless, shivering as they looked for their next meal.

The contrast between rich and poor became a painful reality for Mary. Her employers sat in the warmth of their mansions, day after day, refusing to acknowledge that people were suffering. Why should she sit and sew for people who cared for little aside from their pretty gowns and jewelry?

As the days passed, Mary became more and more frustrated with the injustices she witnessed every day. She knew she lived in a time when workers' rights were overlooked. Mary wanted to help, but she also knew she couldn't do it alone.

It took a second tragedy to transform Mary from a troubled bystander to a fighter for justice. In 1871 Mary Jones lost everything in the Great Chicago Fire. Her shop, her home, and all her possessions were destroyed.

Overnight, Mary was as poor as the people she used to watch each day, except that she knew firsthand that no one really cared. Remembering her husband, she thought of all he had taught her about unions and workers' rights. It became clear: she must get involved in the labor movement.

Mary Harris Jones lost everything in the Great Chicago Fire of 1871.

Mary's New Home:
Wherever Workers Needed Her

After the fire, Mary began to attend meetings of the newly formed Knights of Labor. After a while, she started traveling across the country to support workers' struggles wherever they happened to break out.

Mary lived with workers in tents or shantytowns, getting to know their troubles and their hopes. In turn, workers were heartened by Mary's compassion and **staunch** fighting spirit. Soon, workers were turning to her for leadership. In Kansas City, she organized a group of unemployed men to march on Washington D.C. and demand jobs. In Birmingham, Alabama, she organized coal miners—both African-American and white—during a nationwide coal strike.

Whatever workers were fighting for, one thing was constant: Mary brought people together in the hope for a better future. When her own spirits needed lifting, she remembered what her husband George had always told her: "We can make a difference if we fight side by side and look out for one another."

"We march!" Her strong voice carried the declaration through the afternoon breeze to the miners below. She was small, but Mother Jones was full of energy and passion. Soon, the workers responded, cheering loudly and waving their arms in excitement.

A young boy, close to the stage, caught her eye. He couldn't be more than seven years old. His hands were raw. Red skin and scars lined his palms and the tips of his fingers. Mary knew children such as he worked 60 or more hours each week, receiving little pay for their pains. However, the boy didn't seem to care about his beaten hands. He was staring straight at her, eager and full of hope. A smile crept across Jones's face. Slowly at first, and then with more force, the chant began: "Mother! Mother! Mother!"

Eugene Debs, who led the American Railway Union, was imprisoned during the Pullman Strike of 1894.

Workers first began referring to Mary Jones as "Mother" after she organized a great show of support for Eugene Debs, leader of the American Railway Union. Debs had just been released from prison following the Pullman Strike of 1894. Workers at the railroad convention of 1897 saw her as a caring figure—a woman who would look out for them and support their struggle for fair working conditions and wages. To them, she had become a mother. Now, she was "Mother Jones" to all.

The Pullman strike began on May 11, 1894, when the Pullman Car Company cut workers' wages by 25 percent. Outraged at the news, three thousand workers reacted by going on strike, bringing all railroad traffic west of Chicago to a halt. Many of these workers were members of the American Railway Union led by Eugene Debs.

Support for the strike quickly grew. In a few short days, 125,000 workers on 29 different railroads nationwide had stopped working. The railroads responded by going to court. The result? The court said that unless the striking workers returned to work, they would all be fired. Debs ignored this court order, and the strike continued. Eventually, the United States Army broke up the strike.

Debs was dragged into court, found guilty of defying a court order, and imprisoned for six months. When he was released, he was seen as a hero by workers across the United States. Many of these workers had been organized by Mother Jones. By supporting Debs and the Pullman strike, the labor movement had made a strong statement: We will stick together.

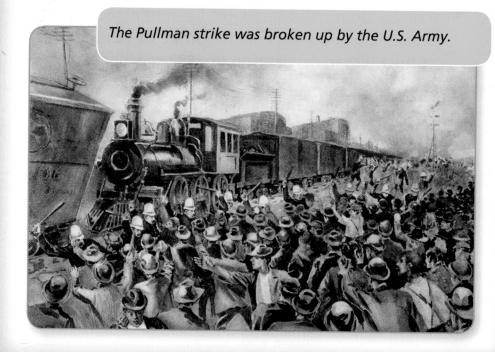

The Pullman strike was broken up by the U.S. Army.

By 1916, newspapers and magazines were beginning to print stories and cartoons about inhumane working conditions for children in U.S. factories.

Standing Up for Children

At the dawn of the twentieth century, conditions among American silk workers were **deplorable**. The workday was long and brutal. Finally, in what became known as the Paterson Silk Strike, they walked off the job. The 100,000 workers—including 16,000 children—demanded that their workweek be cut from 60 to 55 hours. Jones, who wanted to bring the issue of child labor to the public eye, organized a support march. The children's march of 1903, led by Mother Jones, became a powerful moment in the history of American labor.

Children's March from Philadelphia to New York in 1903

"Mother, Mother..." After the chant had died out, the workers returned to their homes to prepare for the march. Early the next morning, they once again met by the wooden stage for the march from Philadelphia to New York City. Mother Jones knew this was just the sort of dramatic statement that these poor workers needed. Jones walked to the front of the group, facing east. Putting one foot in front of the other, the first steps of an 81-mile march began.

In each town they passed, people stopped to stare. Here was a group of textile workers, 100 of them children, led by an old lady with white hair. The marchers continued, the rhythm of their determined steps echoing off houses, firm and **resolute**: Ba-DUM, dum, Ba-DUM, dum, Ba-DUM...

After more than a day of walking, the marchers had arrived at their destination. Many of the workers had never been to New York City, and they were

awed by its size. They spent that second day striding through the city, making their presence known to New York millionaires. Jones remembered sewing for rich Chicago families and watching workers on the streets. She couldn't help but wonder if, at this very moment, anyone was looking out at them from their **lavish** homes. If so, they would see 100 children in torn clothing, dirt staining their faces, all seeking help.

"Mother?" Jones looked down and saw a young boy staring back at her. He handed her a gray stone. Bringing it close to her face, she saw that on it he had carved a face: two round eyes, and one large smile. She put it in the pocket of her dress and smiled down at him. "Thank you," he told her. Jones and the children didn't stop in New York. They walked all the way to President Theodore Roosevelt's Long Island home, their steps even louder now: Ba-DUM, dum...

Mother Jones was one of the first people in the United States to raise the issue of child labor. In 1904, shortly after the march, the National Child Labor Committee was formed. This group began a national campaign to reform federal child labor laws. It was to be just the beginning of a long fight for children's rights in the workplace. Twice, movements to set child labor standards failed to gather enough support.

It wasn't until 1938, eight years after Mother Jones's death, that the government finally enacted the Fair Labor Standards Act. This law **regulated** child labor by establishing a minimum wage, overtime pay, and age requirements for youth employment. The march Jones organized may not have brought about immediate success, but it became the spark that would bring about change.

Until the Fair Labor Standards Act of 1938, no laws protected children who labored in American mines such as this.

Mother Jones leads a march to protest sending troops to the labor strike in Denver, Colorado.

A Dangerous Life

Although Mary Harris became a "mother" to workers nationwide, not everyone received her warmly. Her organizing stirred people up wherever she traveled. Whether in the company towns of West Virginia or the coal camps of Colorado, many did their best to stop Mother Jones from fighting. She was banished from more towns and held in more prisons than any other organizer of her time. One U.S. district attorney went so far as to declare her "the most dangerous woman in America."

Jones knew that her position at the forefront of the labor movement put her at extreme risk. Often, she feared someone might try to cause her physical harm. In one town or the next, she could be beaten—or even shot. In 1912 Mother Jones was arrested for her actions in West Virginia and held under house arrest. At first, she was discouraged: a short stay in jail was one thing, but being held **indefinitely** was difficult. She often sewed to pass the time, but even that became tiresome. Sometimes, it seemed as if she would spend the rest of her life inside.

However, after a few weeks, people began to take action, demanding that she be released. The public show of support was so strong that the state of West Virginia had no choice but to release her. Being jailed was certainly an unpleasant experience. Jones knew, however, that if the authorities went to such great lengths to silence her, it was because her voice was loud and strong. For that, she was proud.

The passion that burned within Mother Jones did not decrease with age. In 1921, when Jones was well into her 80s, she settled in Washington, D.C. and later, on a farm in Maryland. Her desire to serve still made her restless. *More can be done,* she thought, so she continued to travel, aiding in causes when she could. It was three years later, in 1924, that she made her last strike appearance.

In 1928 Mother Jones settled in rural Maryland at the farm of her friend Lillie May Burgess.

It was a cold, windy day in Chicago. For a moment, Mother Jones thought back to the years when she was a young girl with her own dress store here, just starting out in life. Then she looked out at the crowd of dressmakers on strike for fair work standards and better wages. They had struggled for four long months to be heard, and hundreds of them had been arrested.

Mother Jones got up from her chair, and immediately, as if on cue, the strikers hushed. Her right hand rested on a cane, her fragile legs barely able to hold her weight. Jones tried to lift her hand, but it began to shake, pulsing with pain that spread up her arm. She looked out at the faces of the dressmakers.

She needed to do this, but her hands, which once sewed so easily, would now barely obey her commands. Then suddenly, her arm shot up. Valiantly, she raised the cane high above her head. The crowd erupted, hooting and hollering with joy. At this moment, Mother Jones was still a dressmaker. She gripped her cane as tightly as she had once gripped her needle. The familiar chant began, "Mother, Mother, Mother ..."

Although Mary Harris Jones had lost her children, she would forever be a mother to millions.

Mother Jones, 1918

Now Try This

Create a Leadership Profile

What leader do you admire for serving others or standing up for their rights? Is it someone you're familiar with from the news, the Internet, or your reading? Is it a person you know from your family or community? Is this leader a historical figure, or someone from the present day? Identify a leader. Then create a leadership profile that describes him or her.

1. Brainstorm possible leaders by free-writing, browsing the Internet, or talking with one or more classmates. After you select someone, identify this person in a sentence or two.

2. Sketch out a personality profile that answers the following questions:
   • Why do you admire this person?
   • What are some of his or her major accomplishments?
   • How has this person helped others?
   • What obstacles has this person encountered, and how did he or she overcome them?
   • What character traits do you think enable this person to serve others?

3. Look over your notes, and circle what stands out as especially important. Then, plan how you will share your profile with others. Be creative! Use your own special skills and talents—for writing, drawing, collage work, photography, video, or computers—to choose a format. For example, you could write a poem or short essay, compile a résumé, draw a picture, create a poster or collage, or make a video. If you decide to use visuals, include captions.

4. Exchange your profile with a partner, or share it with a group or class. Compare your choice with others, and discuss the different ways these leaders have served others.

Glossary

deplorable *adj.* miserable

famine *n.* extreme, wide scarcity of food

humane *adj.* characterized by tenderness and sympathy for others

indefinitely *adj.* in a way that has no exact limit

lavish *adj.* overly luxurious

oppressive *adj.* unjustly harsh

regulated *v.* controlled by rules or standards

resolute *adj.* determined

staunch *adj.* firm, steadfast, or loyal